古い家並みも残るポンソンビー・ロードは
お洒落なカフェやバー、雑貨店などが並ぶ　1

カランガハペ・ロード（通称 K'Road）の St. Kevins Arcade には
素敵なカフェや古書店がある　2

3 フラットホワイトはオセアニア発祥のエスプレッソ版カフェオレ

4 オークランド市内中心部の対岸に位置するデボンポートのパブ Patriot

ニューマーケットにある TASCA はスペイン料理のお店　5

青い空、長く白い雲の下でカヤックを楽しむ人たち。
背景に見えるのはランギトト島　6

7　デボンポートのヴィクトリア・ストリート沿いにある古書店 BookMark

8　デボンポートの入り口に立つ 1903 年創業のエスプラネード・ホテル

LET US FRESHEN UP YOUR PARTY

 st pierres sushi

FIFTH AVENUE MENSWEAR 216

St. Pierre's は 1993 年から寿司を販売している人気チェーン店　9

  TAKE A SEAT. LITERALLY. FREE !

ポンソンビー・ロードにある古書店 The Open Book の
入り口にちょっと楽しい貼り紙が…　10

No ID
No Service
No Exceptions

Auckland Regional Public Health Service
Rātonga Hauora ā Iwi o Tamaki Makaurau

11　未成年者へのアルコールの提供は厳禁！断固たる掲示！

Cultural Crossroads

—多文化の交差点 New Zealand—

Akira Inoue

Shinako Imaizumi

Christopher Connelly

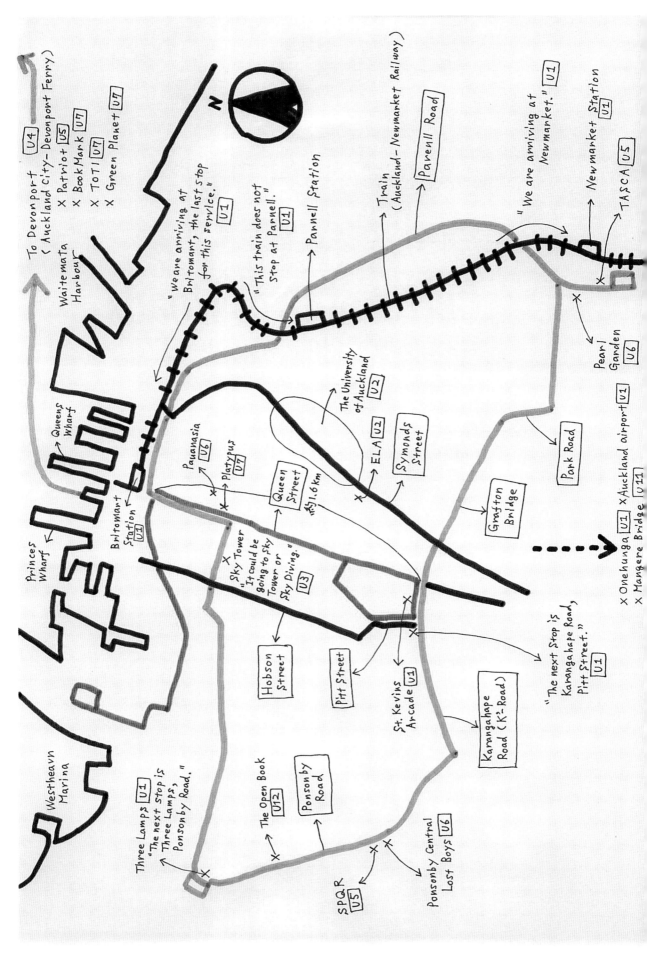

はじめに

ニュージーランド最大の都市であり、人口の約 40 パーセントが海外出身者で
あるといわれているオークランド。そこに、英語研修のため学生を引率して訪れ
ているうちに、オークランドがまさに「多文化の交差点」であることを体感して
きました。そこから生まれたのが本書です。

オークランドを舞台とするこのテキストに登場してくれる人たちの出身地は、
ニュージーランド、イギリス、カナダ、韓国、スロバキア、イタリア、フランス、
ロシア、中国（登場順）と実に多彩です。その意味では、ニュージーランド第 2
の都市であり、「イングランド以外でもっともイングランドらしい街」と言われて
いるクライストチャーチとは対照的です。

テキストの内容も、現地であつめた音、映像、声、新聞記事などから構成され
ており、どこからはじめてもオークランドが多文化の交差点であることを教室内
で体感することができると確信しています。

本テキストの作成にあたり、オークランド大学附属 English Language
Academy ディレクター、Julie Haskel 氏、Jennifer Wright 氏をはじめと
する、たくさんのオークランドの方々にご協力いただきました。記して感謝申し
上げます。

2019 年 9 月

井 上　彰
今 泉　志 奈 子
Christopher Connelly

Kia Ora!
（マオリ語で「こんにちは！」）

本書の使い方

どこからでも、何度でも

本書は全 12 ユニットから構成されています。まずはウォーミングアップとして、バスや郊外電車に乗ってオークランドのあちこちに出かけることをテーマとした Unit 1、オークランド大学附属 English Language Academy の方々が学生さんへのメッセージや留学についての具体的なアドバイスを寄せてくださっている Unit 2, Unit 3 からはじめていただくことをオススメしますが、それ以外のユニットについては、どこから、どの順番で学んでいただいても構いません。授業の目標や、みなさんの興味・関心に応じて、学んでみたいユニットを自由にピックアップしてください。各ユニットの音声データは英宝社ウェブサイトからダウンロード可能です。さらに現地の息づかいを伝える動画データはYouTubeで何度でも再生していただくことができます。授業のあとも、是非、くりかえしこれらのデータを活用して、どこからでも、何度でも、楽しみながら学んでください。

リスニングからはじめたい方は…

Unit 1 はバスや郊外電車のアナウンス音声ですが、Unit 2 ～ 7、Unit 9 は、実際のインタビュー音声をつかっています。つまり現地の人たちの「生の声」をつかったリスニングのユニットです。年齢、職業はもちろん、出身地も様々で、オークランド生まれではない人たちもたくさんいます。是非、多文化空間にあふれる母語話者と非母語話者の英語の両方に触れてください。なかにはことばに詰まったり、言い間違いをしたり、途中で考えがかわって言い替えたりする場面もでてきます。そういった普段着の英語を体感していただくためのユニットです。

リーディングからはじめたい方は…

Unit 8, 10-11 は、現地の新聞 New Zealand Herald の記事をつかったリーディングのユニットです。オークランドの移民社会やマオリ文化に関するもので、ひとつずつ精読することでオークランド社会の現在を感じていただけると思います。なお、本書の記事は、①句読点の表記等における不統一、②数字、表現等がウェブ版とは異なっている箇所が一部にみられますが、これは紙面のままに記載しているためです。ご了承ください。

留学準備・資格試験対策にも

またどのユニットでも、キーワード・キーフレーズをまとめた単語・熟語リスト、空所補充型の英作文問題をつけてありますので、基本的な文法事項を復習しながら無理なく語彙を増やすことができます。留学準備のため、また各種資格試験の準備にも活用してください。

思うところをことばに

最後に、各ユニットには【異文化理解】というセクションがついています。それぞれのユニットで学習したことをもとに、クラスで、グループで自由に討論するための素材です。ディスカッションのトピックとポイントを簡単に挙げてありますので、こちらを自由に活用して、多文化が交差するオークランドが私たちに見せてくれる、様々なことば、社会、文化事象について意見を交換してみてください。ディスカッションは日本語でも、英語でもよいと思います。

語学研修でも、留学でも、ワーキングホリディでも、インターンシップでも、海外に一歩を踏み出し、多文化の空間のなかで学び、働こうと思うなら、「ことばにして思うところを伝える」ことが不可欠です。黙って様子を見ていたり、相手が察してくれるのを待っていたりするだけでは何もはじまりません。実は、海外に渡って日本人学生の多くが一番戸惑うのが、この部分なのです。最初は「そう思う」「そうは思わない」だけでもかまいません。本書の【異文化理解】のセクションを活用して、自ら発言する、少しずつ思うことをことばにして伝えることに慣れ、その楽しみを味わってほしいと思っています。

Best Wishes!

• Auckland

Contents

Welcome to New Zealand!

ニュージーランド最大の都市オークランド市内を一回りするには、メイン・ストリートである長いクイーン・ストリート (Queen Street) を南北に繋ぐ CityLink bus (赤色) や、観光名所であるポンソンビー (Ponsonby) やパーネル (Parnell) を通る InnerLink bus (緑色) がお薦めです。また少し郊外に行くには郊外電車も利用できます。もっとも日本の大都市圏の JR や私鉄の路線網とは比較になりませんが。まずはバスや郊外電車の車内アナウンスを聞き取ってみましょう。

 1-1 CityLink & InnerLink buses

InnerLink bus の車窓から撮影。映像が始まってすぐに、対向車線から赤色の CityLink bus が走ってきます。映像の最後で信号待ちをしていると、隣の車線に後から来た CityLink bus が停車します。まずは InnerLink bus のアナウンスを聞き取ってみましょう。機械音声ですから聞き取りやすいはずです。

> ### Announcements of InnerLink bus

 1 **Three Lamps_Ponsonby Road**

The next stop is Three Lamps; Ponsonby Road. To ensure this service runs to timetable, this bus may wait for a few minutes before continuing.

古い家並みも残る Ponsonby Road

🎧 2 Karangahape Road_Pitt Street

The next stop is Karangahape Road; Pitt Steet. To ensure this service runs to timetable, this bus may wait for a few minutes before continuing.

K'Road の St. Kevins Arcade　中には素敵なカフェや古書店がある

Words & Phrases

Ponsonby Road【お洒落】ポンソンビー・ロード　オークランド市内中心部の西側にあって、北から南に長く伸びる通り。市内中心部からはInnerLink busでアクセス可能。通り沿いにはお洒落なカフェやレストラン、バーやクラブ、それにアンティークショップなど様々な雑貨店があります。

this service 今乗車しているバス（の便）　service（バス・列車などの）便

run （バス・列車が）定期的に運行する

to timetable 時刻表通りに　to=…にあわせて、…通りに

Karangahape Road【庶民的・やや危】カランガハペ・ロード　通称、K-ロード (K'Road)。ポンソンビー・ロードの南端とつながっていて、そこから東に長く伸び、その沿道には様々な種類の店が並んでいます。この道路の一角にはかつて赤線地帯がありましたが、その面影は今ではほとんど残っていません。

次は郊外電車の車内アナウンスです。これも機械音声なので聞き取りやすいと思います。

Train Announcements

🎧 3 The next station is Newmarket

The next station is Newmarket. This train does not stop at Parnell. Please change at Newmarket for Southern line services to Parnell. If there is an emergency, please use the emergency alarm button located next to all doors. Your AT HOP card or ticket may be checked at any time.

Only we ride for free!

Words & Phrases

Newmarket【高級】 ニューマーケット
市内中心部の東南側に位置し、洋服や靴を
扱うお店が立ち並ぶ商業地区。InnerLink
bus でアクセス可能ですが、市内中心部の
ブリトマート駅 (Britomart Station p. 5 の
Words & Phrases を参照) から郊外電車に
乗れば 1 駅 (実際は途中にパーネル駅があ
りますが、アナウンスにある通り、この駅
を通過する電車が多い) です。

Newmarket Station

Parnell【高級】 パーネル　市内中心部の東、上記ニューマーケットの北側に位置しています。歴史的
景観が保存された地区で、パーネル・ロード沿いにはアンティークショップ、雑貨店、カフェやレス
トランが軒を連ねています。

Southern line services　(郊外電車の) 南線の便

AT HOP card　エイ・ティー・ホップ・カード
日本の ICOCA、PiTaPa、Suica 等と同じ交
通系 IC カード。このカード 1 枚あれば、バ
スと郊外電車は言うまでもなく、フェリー
にも利用できるので、オークランド市内の
交通機関は、小銭を心配せずに乗り回すこ
とができます。その一方で、今でもバスに
乗車する際に運転手に紙幣で運賃を支払う
乗客も少なくないし、運転手も嫌な顔をせ
ずに「気長に」お釣りを渡しています。東
京や大阪だと考えられない光景。

AT HOP card

4 Arriving at Newmarket

We are now arriving at Newmarket. Change here for Onehunga and Southern line services. To open the door, press the green button when lit.

5 The next station is Onehunga

The next station is Onehunga; the last stop for this service.

6 We are now arriving at Onehunga

We are now arriving at Onehunga; the last stop for this service. Change here for bus services to Auckland airport. Please make sure you take all your belongings with you. Remember to tag off with your AT HOP card or keep your ticket until you leave the station. To open the door, press the green button when lit. For upcoming events and closures on the rail network that may affect your travel, please visit at.govt.nz.

7 We are now Arriving at Britomart

We are now arriving at Britomart; the last stop for this service. Please make sure you take all your belongings with you. Have your ticket ready for inspection or tag off with your AT HOP card. To open the door, press the green button when lit. For upcoming events and closures on the rail network that may affect your travel, please visit at.govt.nz.

Words & Phrases

We are now arriving at 当列車はまもなく…に到着します
〈語法・文法〉現在進行形を使って「近い未来の予定」を表すことができます。
ex. He is arriving this afternoon. 彼は今日の午後到着する予定です。
またここで使われている "We" は「同じ列車に乗っている私たちは」という意味で、日本語の「（当）列車は」に相当します。
cf. We are open 24 hours. 当店は 24 時間営業です。
Onehunga【庶民的】オネフンガ 市内中心部から 30 番のバスで南へ約 35 〜 40 分。巨大な Dress - Smart というアウトレットモールがあります。
when lit （緑のボタンの）ライトがついてから =When the green button is lit
light=…に明かりをつける

make sure　確実に…する、きっと…する　cf. ensure

ex. Make sure you get there ten minutes early. 必ず 10 分前には到着しておくように。

remember to　忘れずに…する

ex. Remember to call me when you arrive!　着いたら忘れずに連絡してね。

tag off　タグオフする、電子タグ付けを外す

元来 tag は「付け札」の意味で、name tag（名札）、price tag（値札）のように用います。
逆にバスや電車に乗る時は tag on する必要があります。
Use your AT HOP card to tag on before you board your train or ferry and as you board your bus, then tag off when you finish your trip. If you don't tag on and tag off you may be charged the default fare. (at.govt.nz)

keep　…をずっと持っている

ex. I keep all his letters. 彼からの手紙は全部捨てずに持っています。

closure　（鉄道網の）封鎖、閉鎖

Britomart　ブリトマート　オークランドの中心業務地区 (central business district [CBD]) で、バス、郊外電車、そしてフェリーの発着地でもあります。

ready for　…への備えができて

ex. I'm ready for anything. 私はどんなことにも対処する備えができている。何があっても驚かない。

inspection　検札 (ticket inspection)

AT HOP card はコンビニで買えるし、カードにチャージする (top up) ことも可能

バスを降りる際は必ず tag off

情報
　　　市内中心部ブリトマート（北）から、ここで紹介したポンソンビー・ロード（西）→カランガハペ・ロード（南）→ニューマーケット→パーネル（東）の順に InnerLink bus で回るなら、反時計回りの InnerLink bus に乗車すれば OK。逆（時計回り）も当然可。

本文中で使われている単語を用いて英文を完成させましょう。

1. シートベルトをしっかり締めたか確認してください。

   Please [　　　　　　] [　　　　　　　　] your seat belt is securely fastened.

2. バスから降りるときに必ずタグオフするように。

   [　　　　　　　] to tag off as you get off your bus.

3. 列車の中にバッグを置き忘れた (バッグを持たずに降りてしまった)。

   I forgot to [　　　　　　] my bag with me when I got off the train.

4. 夜の10時を過ぎるとこの辺はバスがありません。

   There's no bus [　　　　　　] available here after ten o'clock in the evening.

5. まもなくブリトマート終点に着きます。

   Now [　　　　　] are arriving at Britomart, the last stop for this [　　　　　　　].

6. バスに乗る際にはタグオンしてください。

   Please tag on as you [　　　　　　] your bus.

7. 領収書はすべて取っておいてください。

   You should [　　　　　] all your receipts.

8. その契約は署名を待つばかりだ (いつでも署名できる)。

   The contract is [　　　　　] [　　　　　　] signing.

異文化理解

オークランド市内中心部をグルっと回りましたが、たくさんの地名や道路名が出てきました。クイーン・ストリート (Queen Street) やニューマーケット (Newmarket) といった「いかにも」という名前と、カランガハペ・ロード (Karangahape Road) やオネフンガ (Onehunga) といった「聞きなれない」名前が混在しています。その理由を考えてみましょう。

Language school (1)

Unit 2と Unit 3では、オークランド大学付属イングリッシュ・ランゲージ・アカデミー (The University of Auckland English Language Academy [以下 ELA])のスタッフの方々からの、オークランド (ニュージーランド) で語学研修を計画している日本人学生に向けたメッセージを聞いてみましょう。ニュージーランドは多民族国家であるとよく言われますが、メッセージを寄せてくださった ELA の2人のスタッフの出身はイギリスとカナダです。両方のメッセージに、多様性を表す "different" "differences" という言葉が使われています。また最初のメッセージでは "brave" という言葉が、そして2番目のメッセージでは「あらゆる機会 (opportunities) をとらえて」という表現が繰り返されています。現地では、勇気を出して、あらゆる機会をとらえて、様々な場所で様々な国籍の人に英語で話してみましょう。

まず、イギリス出身のジュリー (Julie Haskel) のメッセージを聞いてみましょう。

Julie Haskel@English Language Academy (UK)

🎧 8 My name is Julie

(So, Julie, could you please introduce yourself?)
OK, Good morning! My name is Julie, Julie Haskel. I'm the director of the English Language Academy in Auckland.

🎧 9 My advice would be

(So Julie, could you give some advice for the Japanese students wishing to study in New Zealand, in particular, at the English Language Academy?)
OK, I think my advice would be for students to come with an open mind and to enjoy the differences and every day to be brave and to try something new; whether it's new food or to go to a different beach or a different museum and to really make the most of their time; take lots of photos and make lots of friends and be brave, speak English!

ELA 初日のオリエンテーション

最終日の授業評価風景

Words & Phrases

my advice would be 私がアドバイスするとしたら…になるでしょうね。
〈語法・文法〉would は仮定法過去形で「もしそれが許されるなら」とか「仮にそのようなことになれば」といった仮定の気持ちが含まれていて、丁寧で遠慮がちな意向や推量を表わします。
ex. I would stay home all day today: It is horribly cold outside. 私なら今日は一日中家にいますね。外はものすごく寒いですよ。

make the most of …をできるだけ (有効に) 利用する
ex. Make the most of what you have. あなたが持っているものを最大限活用しなさい。

次に、カナダ出身のジェニファー (Jennifer Wright) からのアドバイスを聞いてみましょう。

Jennifer Wright@English Language Academy (Canada)

 10 My name is Jennifer

(So, Jennifer, could you please introduce yourself?)
Certainly! My name is Jennifer Wright. I'm the director of studies at the University of Auckland English Language Academy. So my role is I'm responsible for all of the academic programs, all of the teaching staff and the quality assurance of the teaching and learning.

Words & Phrases

Certainly! もちろん (いいですよ)、承知しました。
ex. May I ask you a question? Certainly! 質問してもいいですか。ええ、どうぞ。
cf. Certainly not! とんでもない。

the director of studies 教育部門の長　director は「長」を意味する語なので、学校長であるジュリーの自己紹介においても、部門の長であるジェニファーの自己紹介においても同じ語が出てきます。しかし、ふたりの発音には違いが見られます。イギリス出身のジュリーは、director という語を [daɪréktə] と発音していたのに対し、カナダ出身のジェニファーは、[dəréktə] と発音していますね。

11 **Absolutely!**

(So,...um...could you give some advice for the Japanese students wishing to study in New Zealand, especially...um...at the English Language Academy, please?)

Absolutely! Um...for students, Japanese students, or any students in fact, who are planning to study at the University of Auckland English Language Academy, they need to take advantage of all of the opportunities that are offered both inside and outside of the classroom because, as I said, learning doesn't stop when the class finishes. So what I mean by that is inside the classroom we have students from many different nationalities and students want to take all the opportunities they can to try to meet students of other nationalities. So when it's...there's a break time, to try not to just spend the break time with their friends from their own Japanese university but to try to go and to have a coffee with someone from another country or at least...an...a different Japanese university.

Words & Phrases

um   えー、あー、うーん　日常の会話では、次に何を言うか躊躇しているときの発声（間投詞 [interjection]）が入る方がむしろ自然です。この教科書は、インタビューや実際の会話のシーンの中の間投詞をそのままの形で残しています。

ex. Um, I guess so. うーん、私もそう思います。

Absolutely!   もちろん！ cf. certainly

are planning to study   勉強するつもりである　plan to do には「すでにはっきりと〜をする計画があること」が暗示されています。

ex. I'm planning to buy a new car.   新車を買うつもりである（新車購入計画がすでに立っている）。

cf. I'm thinking of buying a new car. 新車を買おうかと考えている。

take advantage of   （機会を）利用する

ex. Take advantage of today's special offer.   本日の特別価格でのご提供をお見逃しなく。

What I mean by that is...   =What I mean by that is that...

それはどういうことかと言うと…ということです

mean= …のつもりで言う、…と言おうとしている

cf. What do you mean by that? それはどういうことですか。

take all the opportunities they can to   あらゆる機会をとらえて…する

ex. You must take this opportunity to show what you can do. この機会をとらえて君の実力を見せなさい。

to try not to do…but to try to do...   …しないで、…すること（が大切です）

本文中で使われている単語を用いて英文を完成させましょう。

1. この計画の責任者は誰ですか。

   Who's [   ] for this project?

2. 利用できるあらゆる機会をとらえなさい。

   [   ] every opportunity available.

3. 彼は議長の任を果たした。

   He filled the [   ] of chairman.

4. 私が言わんとすることは、ここで待っていても意味がないということだ。

   What I [   ] is that there's no point in waiting here.

5. オリンピック競技で一番大切なことは勝つことではなく、参加することである。

   The most important thing in the Olympic Games is [   ] to win
   [   ] to take part.

6. 彼に会うつもりはない。

   I do not [   ] to meet him.

7. 元気 (勇気) を出しなさい。

   Be [   ] !

8. 私たちは言われた通りにした。

   We did [   ] we were told.

9. 今日一日休んでもいいですか。（もちろん）いいですよ。

   Can I have a day off today? [   ].

10. 今日一日休んでもいいですか。とんでもない。

    Can I have a day off today? [   ] not.

10

**——基礎編**

ELAで1カ月の英語研修プログラムに参加することになったら、いつ（何月）に行きたいと思いますか。それはなぜですか。

クラスで出会った外国人留学生に、日本について質問されたら、英語でこたえられますか？まず、下記のリストをつかって、チェックしてみましょう。

1) 日本のどこ（どの地域）出身なの？
   (Which part of Japan are you from?)
   (Which prefecture in Japan are you from?)
   (Which city in Japan are you from?)

2) あなたの出身地は日本のどのあたりにあるの？
   (In which part of Japan is your hometown located?)
   (Where in Japan is your hometown located?)

3) あなたの出身地は何で有名なの？特産品はある？
   (What is your hometown famous for? Any local specialties?)

4) 日本の人口は？あなたの出身地の人口は？
   (How many people are there in Japan? How about your hometown?)

5) あなたの大学には学生が何人くらいいるの？先生は何人くらい？
   (How many students does your university have? How many teachers/professors?)

**——応用編**

クラスメートの留学生から訊ねられるかもしれない質問をいくつか用意しました。どこまで英語でこたえられますか？

1) 日本人ってどうして毎日バスタブにつかるの？
   (Why do Japanese people take a bath every day?)

2) 日本に行くとしたら、東京と京都、どっちに先に行くべき？
   (When I travel to Japan, where should I visit first, Tokyo or Kyoto?)

3) オススメのアニメ、おしえて！
   (Could you / Can you recommend me your favorite *anime*, please?)
   (What's your favorite *anime*?)

Language school (2)

ひきつづき、ELA のスタッフで、教育部門の長であるジェニファー (Jennifer) からのアドバイスを聞いてみます。この Unit では、特に授業中に学んだ英語を、ニュージーランドでの留学生活においてどのように活かしていくか、クラスの外での学びについてのアドバイスです。

Jennifer Wright@English Language Academy (Canada)

12 Activities outside of the classroom

Also at the ELA, we have a University of Auckland student who comes up here every week who runs activities outside of the classroom. And these activities are varied; it could be doing...um...playing football or doing...a...table tennis tournament here or it could be going to the Sky Tower or Sky Diving, it could be many different things. This is a great way for students to meet other students in the school and really widen their network of friends and really use that English that they've used in class and extend it outside and to really learn about New Zealand culture and take on board all of that.

3-1 Sky Tower から見たオークランド大学周辺

Sky Tower から見たオークランド大学　中央にあるのがオークランド大学の象徴的建造物である The Clock Tower

今から Sky Jump に挑戦する女性

Words & Phrases

We have a University of Auckland student

情報 語学学校は大きく分けて民間の語学学校と大学附属の語学学校の2種類があります。ELA はオークランド大学附属の語学学校なので、このインタビューにもあるように、オークランド大学の学生が ELA に来て様々なアクティビティ（課外活動）の運営に関わっています。このように大学附属の語学学校の場合は、その大学の学生と交流することも可能なわけです。その一方で大学附属の語学学校の場合、その大学に正式に入学する留学生のみを（あるいは優先的に）受け入れる傾向が最近強くなってきました。

run 〈他動詞〉…を経営する、切り盛りする、催す、提供する
ex. The college runs summer courses for foreign students. 大学は外国人学生向けに夏期講習会を設けている。

varied 様々な　変化にとんだ
cf. The prices vary with size. 値段はサイズによっていろいろ。

could ひょっとしたら…かもしれない
ex. One day he could be famous, but the chances are very small. ひょっとしたら彼はいつか有名になるかもしれないが、その可能性は極めて低い。

Sky Tower オークランド中心部にそびえる 328 メートルの南半球一高いタワー　Sky Diving（正式な名称は Sky Jump）は Sky Tower から命綱を付けて飛び降りるアトラクション

take on board all of that take...on board …を受け入れる、理解する　本来は「…を船内（機内）に積み込む」という意味。ここでは…の部分（all of that）が後ろに来ていることに注意。
cf. Several Russians were with us on board. 同じ機にロシア人が何人か搭乗していた。

🎧 13 ▶ **Homestay**

And finally, of course, for the students who are staying in a homestay, a... New Zealand homestay, this is an opportunity of a lifetime because this is learning 24 hours a day. You can have breakfast with your homestay family and talk about what you're going to do for the day, how you're going to get to school, what bus you're going to take, you can talk at dinner about what you did, what your homework is. Try to use the learning from the class that day together with your homestay family, play with the children if they have children, spend time with your homestay family doing the things that Kiwi families love to do at the weekend.

500 番のバスで市内中心部から南東方向にあるホームステイ先の Greenlane へ約 30 分

典型的なホームステイ先の周辺

Words & Phrases

- **have breakfast** 朝食をとる　eat も使えますが、eat は、本来「食べ物を口に入れて、咀嚼し飲み込む」という意味なので、「食事をとる」という場合は、have を使うほうが自然です。
  cf. What did you eat for breakfast ?　朝食に何を食べましたか?
- **get to** …に着く　cf. I got home around half past nine.　9 時半ごろに家に着いた。
- **take** …に乗る、…を利用する
- **together with** …と共に、…に加えて、
- **Kiwi** もともと kiwi はニュージーランドの国鳥のキーウィ(キウイ)のことですが、Kiwi で「ニュージーランド人」の意味
- **love to do** …するのが大好きである
  ex. Kids love to hear fairy tales.　子供はおとぎ話を聞くのが大好きだ。

EXCERCISES 空所補充

本文中で使われている単語を用いて英文を完成させましょう。

1. あのレストランの経営はうまくいっている。
   The restaurant is well [　　　　　　].

2. 大学へ行くにはどのバスに乗ったらいいんですか。
   [   ] bus should I [   ] to go to the university?

3. 駅前から 52 番のバスに乗ってください。
   [   ] the number 52 bus from in front of the station.

4. 彼はカードを添えて彼女にバラの花を贈った。
   He sent her some roses [   ] with a card.

5. 電話に出てくれませんか。ひょっとしたら僕のボスからかもしれないので。
   Will you answer the phone? It [   ] be my boss.

6. ここから警察署へはどうやったら行けますか。
   How can I [   ] to the police station from here?

7. 様々な課外活動を提供します。
   We provide a wide variety of outdoor [   ].

8. 家族と一緒にハワイでクリスマスを過ごした。
   I [   ] Christmas in Hawaii with my family.

9. 毎朝 7 時に朝食です。
   We [   ] breakfast at seven.

10. 我々はビジネスを中国にまで広げる計画である。
    We are planning to [   ] our business to China.

異文化理解 ——基礎編

ELA で 1 カ月の英語研修プログラムに参加することになったら、授業外では何をしてみたいと思いますか。ELA のウェブサイトやニュージーランド（オークランド）の観光スポットなどを調べて、「挑戦してみたいことリスト」をつくってみましょう。

異文化理解 ——応用編

ニュージーランドでホームステイすることになった場合を想定して、これからあなたのホストファミリーになるご家族に向けて、自己紹介をかねた簡単な手紙を書いてみましょう。
＊実際に、ELA に入学し、ホームステイを希望する場合、ホームステイ申込書に上記のような手紙を添えて提出することが求められます。

Unit 4

At the shops

この Unit では、カフェとアイスクリーム屋さんで注文してみましょう。語学研修の場合、その多くはホームステイで、朝と夜の食事は提供されますが、お昼は「自腹」です。また観光でニュージーランドを訪れている場合は、常に欲しいものは自分で注文しなければなりません。日本のコンビニでも店員さんが外国人ということが珍しくありませんが、ニュージーランドでも同様です。特にこの Unit でとりあげるアイスクリーム屋さんでは、店員は韓国人留学生、客は日本人なので、英語、韓国語、日本語の3か国語が飛び交います。

Staff@Gloria Jean's Coffees

14 Staff at Gloria Jean's Coffees

Staff: Hi!

Tourist 1: Hiya! Um, can we have a small size of um hot tea?

Staff: Small size of what?

Tourist 1: Hot tea...

Staff: What kind of tea did you want, black tea, we've got English breakfast or berry, green tea?

Tourist 2: English breakfast tea.

Staff: English...did you want milk with that?

Tourist 1: No, no, thank you.

Staff: No? Small one?

Tourist 2: Small.

Tourist 1: Yes...and for me small size of um flat white?

Staff: ...flat white, yeah?

Tourist 1: ...and one egg bacon bagel.

Staff: Er...bacon and egg bagel?

Tourist 1: Yes, and for me...um...cheese ham croissant.

Staff: Croissant. Did you want them warmed?

Tourist 1: Ah yes, please!

Staff: Is it to have here or take away?

Tourist 1: Um...here, thank you very much.

Staff: Seventeen-ninety.

Tourist 1: Right.

Staff: Debit card or by cash?

Tourist 1: Ah, cash, please. Here you are.

Staff: Thank you.

Tourist 1: Thank you very much!

Words & Phrases

We've got... （当店には）…があります

berry ベリー系の紅茶

with that それ（紅茶）に、それと一緒に
cf. Does it come with salad? それにはサラダが
つきますか。

flat white フラットホワイト　オセアニア発祥のエ
スプレッソ版のカフェオレ

er えー、えーと、あのー　ex. I...er... 私はですね、
あのー　cf. um

want them warmed それを温めてほしい
"want ...toasted" と言うこともある。
cf. Do you want your coffee black or white?
コーヒーはブラックにしますか、それともミルク
を入れますか。

フラットホワイトと見事なラテアート

Is it to have here or take away? 店内でお召し上がりですか、それともお持ち帰りですか。
"Is it for here or to go?" "For here or to go?" と言うこともできます。

seventeen-ninety 17ドル90セント　日本円で約1,340円（1ニュージーランドドル＝75円で計算）

情報 海外へ行く場合、円とその国の通貨の為替レートによって、懐具合が大きく変わってきます。
ここでは1NZドル＝75円で計算していますが、2000年10月には1NZドル＝42円と
いう時がありました。この時だと17ドル90セントは750円です。逆に2007年には1NZドルが
97円になりました。すると同じ金額でも1,740円と跳ね上がり、その差は実に1,000円にもなり
ます。

debit card デビットカード（利用金額が直接口座から引き落とされる銀行発行のカード）

情報 支払いはデビットカードや現金の他、クレジットカードでも可能。日本ではファストフード
店での支払いをクレジットカードでする人はまだまだ少ないですが、海外ではごく普通。逆
に日本でファストフード店の支払い（千円以下）を1万円札で支払っても何の問題もないですが、海
外では支払いの金額に関わらず、高額紙幣で支払うことは稀で、クレジットカードでの支払いが一
般的です。

Here you are （お金を店員さんに渡しながら）はい、これ。

カフェのペーパーナフキンのメッセージ "TAKE A MOMENT
NOT A SELFIE"
このメッセージはどういう意味かわかりますか？

注文の番号札28番には "What is the start of melting point
for butter in degrees?" というクイズが書かれています。
答えはわかりますか？

では、ここでフェリーに乗って、対岸のデボンポート (Devonport) に移動しましょう。

Staff@Ice cream shop at Devonport

15 **Staff at an ice cream shop at Devonport**

Tourist 1: Hi! ...um can we have um ice cream?

Staff: Sure!

Tourist 1: So... [to Tourist 2] *Dore-ni suru*? This one? Ah...one scoop of After Dinner...

Staff: After Dinner?

Tourist 1: And then...[wondering]

Staff: Just one scoop?

Tourist 1: Ah yes, please. [pause]...And...um...one scoop of ...um...Affogato for me.

Staff: Affogato.

Tourist 1: Yeah.

Staff: Are you guys from Japan?

Tourist 1: Yes, oh you can recognize that?

Staff: Yeah, I can recognize it.

Tourist 1: Where are you from?

Staff: I'm from Korea.

Tourist 1: Ah, yes I can see it as well!

Staff: If you wanna say that you want lots, you say *"Ippai onegai shimasu!"*

Tourist 1: Exactly! Oh, you've got a very good conduct of Japanese. [Staff: Ah...] Have you ever been to Japan?

Staff: No, no, no, no! Um..I just have lots of Japanese friends.

Tourist 1: Ah, yeah... [Staff: Here you are.] So how much in all?

Staff: Uh, that's nine dollars, please.

Tourist 1: Yeah...sorry I don't have a 10 dollar bill!

Staff: That's OK!

Tourist 1: Sorry!

Staff: Here you are.

Tourist 1: Thank you very much and *Gam Sa Ham Ni Da*!

Staff: *Gam Sa Ham Ni Da*! *"Arigato!"*

Tourist 1: *Arigato*!

Words & Phrases

- **Devonport**　デボンポート　詳しくは Unit 5 と Unit 7 を参照
- **one scoop of**　アイスクリームすくい1杯分の　2杯分の時は "two scoops of..." となる。
- **guys**　(性別を問わず) 人たち、連中　ex. Hi, guys! やあ、みんな。
- **from**　…出身の、…生まれの
     ex. Where are you from?　どこ出身ですか。　I'm from Auckland.　オークランド生まれです。
- **wanna**　=want to
- **conduct**　command (自由に使いこなす力) を使うのが正しい言い方です。
     ex. You have a very good command of Japanese.　日本語がたいへんお上手ですね。
- **Here you are**　(店員がお客にアイスクリームを渡しながら) はい、どうぞ。
- **Here you are**　(店員がお客にお釣りを渡しながら)、はい、これ (お釣りです)。

EXCERCISES 会話練習 基礎編

カフェやファストフード店でよく使う台詞をまとめてみました。ペアになって、これらの台詞を使って、店員と客のやり取りを実演してみましょう。

●会話例1) ―注文
　店員さん役＝「何になさいますか。」と声をかけます。
　お客さん役＝お店にはどんな種類のお茶があるか訊きます。
　店員さん役＝お店にあるお茶の種類を提示します。
　お客さん役＝提示されたお茶のなかからグリーンティ (小サイズ) を1つ選びます。
　店員さん役＝それと一緒に何か他に注文は?と訊きます。
　お客さん役＝レモンメレンゲパイを一切れ (a piece of lemon meringue pie) 注文します。

●会話例2) ―どこで食べる?
　店員さん役＝店内で食べるかテイクアウェイするかを確認します。
　お客さん役＝店内で食べると伝えます。

●会話例3) ―支払い
　店員さん役＝全部で8ドル50セントであることを伝え、支払い方法を確認します。
　お客さん役＝現金での支払いを選び、20ドル札しかないことをことわって支払います。
　店員さん役＝お釣りを渡して「どうもありがとうございます。」
　お客さん役＝「ありがとう。」

店員	What would you like? 何になさいますか。	客	Can I have...?　…をください。 I'll have...　私は…にします。 I'd like...　…をください。
客	What kind of...do you have? どんな種類の…がありますか。	店員	We have... (We've got...) 当店には…があります。

店員	Do you want...with that?	**客**	... please (with that).
	それと一緒に…はいりますか（いかがですか）？		…も（一緒に）お願いします。
			No, thank you.
	Anything else?		いいえ結構です（これで全部です）。
	他に何かご注文はありませんか。		That's all.　（注文は）これで全部です。

店員	Is it to have here or take away?	**客**	I'll have it here.　ここで食べます。
	こちらでお召し上がりになりますか、お持ち帰りですか。		For here / Here, please.
			ここで食べます。
	= Is it for here or to go?		I'll take it away.　Takeaway, please.
	= For here or to go?		持ち帰りです。
			To go, please.　持ち帰りです。

店員	Debit card or by cash?	**客**	I'll pay by debit card / credit card / cash.
	デビットカードですか、現金ですか。		私は…で払います。
	Thank you.　ありがとうございます。		Here you are.
			（代金を渡しながら）はい、これ。

店員	Here you are.	**客**	Thank you.　ありがとう。
	（注文の品を渡しながら）はい、どうぞ。		Thanks!　ありがとう。
	Thank you.　ありがとうございました。		Cheers!　ありがとう。

EXCERCISES　会話練習 応用編

基礎編の練習のあとは、注文内容や、食べる場所（店内またはテイクアウェイ）、支払い方法などを自由に設定して、様々な会話のパターンを練習してみましょう。留学先では客の立場になりますが、日本のアルバイト先では、海外からのお客さまをお迎えする店員の立場になる人も少なくないでしょう。この Unit では、是非、両方の立場で自然な会話ができるように練習しておいてください。

Unit 5

Working in New Zealand now

この Unit では、ポンソンビー (Unit 1参照) のイタリアンレストラン、エス・ピー・キュー・アール (SPQR)、市内中心部の対岸に位置するデボンポートのパブ、パトリオット (Patriot)、それからニューマーケット (Unit 1参照) のスペイン料理のお店、タスカ (TASCA) で働いている人たちの声を紹介します。我々の「直撃」インタビューに答えてくれた彼らの出身は、スロバキア、イタリア、フランス、イングランド、ロシアと様々です。イングランド出身者以外はみんな非英語圏から来た人たちですが、すっかりニュージーランドでの生活と仕事に慣れ親しんでいます。6年前に「ロシア」から「ニュージーランド」に来た男性は「スパニッシュ」レストランのマネジャーをしています。我々も見習わなければ。ということで、この Unit の英語は少しおかしいところもありますが、そのまま掲載しています。

 **5-1** @SPQR

Michaela (Slovakia)

16 **Michaela@SPQR**

(Any comments for Japanese students, please?)
Hello, guys! So...I'm er from Slovakia, my name is Michaela, and I arrived to New Zealand two years ago as a student of English. I was meant to stay here for a half year but somehow I fell in love with this country and I stay here longer; it's a beautiful place, open-mind people, beautiful green...er...landscapes, lovely open-heart people, lovely place to come. You must come and to see yourself!

Words & Phrases

arrived to New Zealand　正しくは arrived [　　　　　　　] New Zealand
was meant to stay　be meant to do=…することになっている
　　ex. You are meant to take off your shoes here. ここでは靴を脱ぐことになっています。
open-mind　心の広い、オープンな　正しくは open-[　　　　　]
open-heart　親切な、思いやりのある　正しくは open-[　　　　　]
come and to see　正しくは come and see もしくは、come to see　正しい使い方については、
　　Unit 6 の p. 29 の Words & Phrases を参照

17 Michele@SPQR

Hi, guys! I'm Michele from Italy, I'm here, I'm studying here in New Zealand English and er...I am really enjoying er all this time in SPQR. And er...probably um I'll come back in Italy and I'll continue to study because er knowing the language is always a wonderful stuff.

Words & Phrases

SPQR ポンソンビー・ロード（Unit 1 を参照）にあるイタリアンレストラン
come back in Italy 正しくは come back [　　　　　] Italy

SPQR　夜は大勢のオークランドの人たちが押し寄せてくる。

18 Nicolas@SPQR

Alright, guys! I'm Nicholas. I'm from France and just arrived in er...New Zealand two month ago. Really recommend like this country; it's very nice opportunity for you to study and like learn their...like... Kiwi, Kiwi culture um...just like come... come, and just try it's very good experience.... what else for you guys (Michaela "Keep talking!") OK? It's good, OK? Ah, hahaha....

Words & Phrases

Alright = all right
two month 正しくはもちろん two months
like （ほとんど意味のないつなぎ言葉として）その、あの、例えば
　　ex. She was, like, really worried about you. 彼女は、その、本当に心配してたよ。
what else 他に何か（ぼくが話すことあるかな）
　　cf. Who else is coming?　他に誰が来るんですか。
　　　Anything else?　他に何かご入用のものは（言いたいことは）ありますか。
Keep talking 話し続けるのよ　keep...ing …し続ける

SPQR の人たちと　英語ではなすとすぐ友達に

Rosie (UK)

🎧 19 ▶ Rosie@Patriot

Um, my name's Rosie Whelan, I'm twenty-four years old and I've been working at the Patriot for about four or five months since April... um I'm actually from England and I'm, I'm here on a working holiday visa. So I came to Auckland; came to Devonport, handed out some CVs and that's how I got my job here!

Words & Phrases

Devonport　オークランド市内中心部からフェリーで 12 分のところにあるデボンポート。
　ヴィクトリア・ストリート (Victoria Street) 沿いには古い建物が残り、ホテル、カフェ、パブ、古書店、雑貨屋などが並んでいます。Unit 1 にも書きましたが、このフェリーにも AT HOP card が使えます。
Patriot　デボンポートにあるアイリッシュパブ
handed out　hand out=…を配る、ばらまく
CV　履歴書　CV=curriculum vitae
that's how...　そういうふうにして…する
　ex. That's how it happened.　そういうふうにして事は起こったのです。

Patriot（元 Bank of New Zealand の建物）とその内部

🎧 20 Ilya@TASCA

(Could you give some message for the Japanese students who wish to study in New Zealand?)

Yes, sure! Um...hello, my name is Ilya. And first I came to New Zealand as a, a language student as well; it was about six years ago and um...I stayed here for about three months and I loved New Zealand, so after about a little break, I came back here to study and then I, I stayed...so now I'm uh, managing the restaurant at Newmarket called TASCA. And so come on over and check us for coffee. I hope you're gonna have a good time here and yeah, take care!

Words & Phrases

break 中断 (ここでは一時帰国していたこと)
TASCA ニューマーケット (Unit 1 を参照) にあるスペイン料理のレストラン
over 〈副詞〉こちらへ、話し手の所 (家) へ
   ex. Come over and see us sometime. いつかこちらへお立ち寄りください。
check …を訪問する
gonna = going to
take care 気をつける (別れの挨拶) Take care! 気をつけて、さよなら、じゃあね。

TASCA Restaurant Café and Bar とその内部

本文中で使われている単語を用いて英文を完成させましょう。

1. 何人か今夜うちにくることになっています。
   Some people are coming [   ] tonight.

2. そういうふうに彼はやったんです。
   That's [   ] he did it.

3. つまらない質問ばかりしないでください
   Don't [   ] asking silly questions.

4. なんとなく彼は信頼できません。
   [   ] I don't trust him.

5. 雨は小やみなく降っていました。
   There was no [   ] in the rain.

EXCERCISES 会話練習 基礎編

この Unit では、ニュージーランドにやってきて、今働いている人たちが、それぞれのスタイルで自己紹介をしながら、どのような経緯で今の仕事を得て、どのような目標をもっているかについて語ってくれています。ペア、もしくは 3 〜 4 人のグループをつくり、初対面だという想定でお互いに自己紹介をしてみましょう。
その際に、以下の基本表現を参考にしてみましょう。

❶挨拶＋名前
Hi, my name is...

❷出身
I'm from ...

❸今の自分
I am a University student.
I am studying English at 語学学校などの名称 (例：English Language Academy)
I am majoring in 分野名 (例：sociology, history, politics, literature, linguistics など)
I chose this major/field of study because... 専攻分野を選んだ理由
What I like most about my university/my language school is... 大学 (語学学校) の
   よいところ

❹将来の自分

After graduation, I am planning to.../thinking of...
My future goal is...

EXCERCISES 会話練習 応用編

上記の①〜④は、自己紹介において中心となるポイントを相手にわかりやすく伝えるためのヒントに過ぎません。実際の会話において、「自己紹介はこのようにあるべき」といったルールはありません。名前や出身地、今何をしているかといった基本的な情報を伝えたあとは、話したいことや興味のあることを自由に話そうとする姿勢が大切です。また、聞く側も、あいづちをうつだけでなく、積極的に質問をして、相手から様々な情報を引き出すように工夫しましょう。その際には、Why...? How...? といった wh 句をうまくつかうといいですね。

Why did you decide to study in New Zealand?
（どうしてニュージーランドで勉強することにしたの？）

How do you like Auckland?
（オークランドはどうですか？＝オークランドのどんなところが好きですか？）

What made you so interested in English?
（どうして、そんなに英語に興味をもつようになったの？）

Which parts of/ What places in New Zealand have you already visited?
（これまでにニュージーランドのどこに行った？）

... など

アドバイス♥♥♥

日本の習慣では、初対面の人に対して、あれこれと質問するのは失礼だと思いがちですが、英語圏、とりわけ、ニュージーランドのように、様々な背景をもった人たちが集まって、肩を寄せ合って暮らしている国では、知りたいこと、訊きたいことは、はっきりと口に出して質問するのが、お互いに心近くなるための大切な第一歩。ただ、「うん、うん」とうなずくだけでは、「関心がないのかな？」「話したくないのかな？」という残念な誤解が生じてしまう危険性すらあります。Unit 2 で、ジュリーがアドバイスしてくれていた、"Be Brave!" というメッセージを思い出して、まずは、相手を見て、ことばにして話す、訊くところからはじめましょう！

Unit 6

Local people in Auckland (1)

この Unit では、オークランド市内中心部の雑貨店、パウアネイジア (Pauanesia) の若い店員さんのケイティ (Katie)、ニューマーケットにある老舗の中華料理店、パール・ガーデン (Pearl Garden) の経営者メイベル (Mabel) とその息子さんクリス (Chris)、そして最後にポンソンビーで服屋、ロスト・ボーイズ (Lost Boys) を始めたばかりの青年ジョエル (Joel) にインタビューをしてみました。一人一人の会話の癖が分かると同時に、みんなが共通の認識を持っていることも、彼らが使うことばから見えてきます。

6-1 オークランドの目抜き通り Queen Street を Inner Link Bus で

Katie@Paunesia

🎧 21 Katie@Pauanesia

(So Katie, could you give some message for the Japanese students who wish to study in New Zealand?)

Ah, yes, so...I...work at Pauanesia and we sell a lot of...um...New Zealand made craft and homeware and gifts for people and...um...I studied at Elam School of Fine Arts and...um...New Zealand contemporary art is really interesting. You should definitely check out the Auckland Art Gallery and um...make sure that you...get to know the Maori-culture's important and um...go to the museum and all sorts of things like that, and talk to lots of, lots of Kiwis, they will be very happy to, to tell you all the local places to go to and um...make sure you travel and you definitely look at the countryside and go on to the bush; and make sure you go to the beaches for a swim and do lots of exploring and what else, what else, what else should I say? (Maybe a little bit about your shop finally?) Oh, what about my shop? Don't know what to say, ooh, (Oh, that's OK) um that's alright...um...yeah, make sure...yes, so, enjoy! A-ha-ha-ha! (Great.)

Pauanesia にて

お店で人気の Kiwi birds

Words & Phrases

Pauanesia パウアネイジア　オークランド市内中心部にある雑貨屋さん。地元のアーティストによる手作りオリジナル「キウイ」のぬいぐるみが有名です。

Elam School of Fine Arts　オークランド大学の Creative Arts and Industries 学部の1学科で、前身の Elam School of Art and Design は Dr John Edward Elam の遺贈によって創設されました。

definitely　絶対、なんと言っても

Maori-culture　マオリ文化　マオリ＝ヨーロッパ人の到来以前に、ニュージーランドに居住していたポリネシア人

make sure　Unit 1 の p. 5 の Words & Phrases を参照

get to know　…わかるようになる　get to do＝…にするようになる
　ex. I feel I'm getting to know him. だんだん彼のことがわかってきたような気がする。

lots of　＝ a lot of

happy　（happy to do の形で）喜んで…する
　ex. I shall be happy to accept your invitation. 喜んでご招待をお受けいたします。

Chris@Pearl Garden

22 **Chris@Pearl Garden**

(OK Chris, please!)

Hello students! My name is Chris.　Er...welcome to Auckland!　Um...hope you'll enjoy your stay here.　So the advice I'd give to you, to learn English would probably be to speak to locals, and don't be shy to approach a local, and maybe ask for directions or you know, invest in the conversation!

(And how do you feel about your life in Auckland? Do you [yeah, wel...] like it?)

Oh, I love Auckland, yeah, um, I like the out, outdoor activities. So I like to get outside when I've got, when I've some free time.　Um...I like fishing, ...I like, like a lot of the sports as well. (Thank you!　Thank you very much!)

何世代にもわたってオークランドに暮らし、レストランを経営している中華系の人たち

Words & Phrases

Mabel@Pearl Garden

23 **Mabel@Pearl Garden**

Hello! My name is Mabel Kan and we've got the Pearl Garden restaurant here in Newmarket; It's a...old...um...traditional Chinese restaurant and er...I'd like to welcome anyone who'd like to come to our restaurant; Um, the New Zealanders are usually very friendly and, and helpful, so I hope you enjoy the country, and fresh air and friendly people! And...um...please come and try our food as well. Er...we have lovely dim-sum and Cantonese style dishes for dinner, so I hope you can have time to come and see us! Thank you! (Thank you!)

中国語と英語の看板

Words & Phrases

6-2 2階建てバスに乗って小旅行気分を味わいましょう。

バスは郊外からニューマーケットの中心部に入っていきます。途中緑色の InnerLink bus と 2 回すれ違います。

Joel@ Lost Boys

 Joel@Lost Boys

Auckland is a great place to come; a very busy city...um...here in Ponsonby Central we get quite a lot of people through. Um, Auckland very friendly place,...um...and very diverse cultures coming to Auckland to study; I would definitely highly recommend choosing Auckland, New Zealand to study! (Thank you very much.) Cool! Thank you

ニュージーランドの人たちはとてもフレンドリー

Words & Phrases

busy にぎやかな、繁華な
Ponsonby Central ポンソンビー・セントラル　ポンソンビーにある、レストランやカフェ、雑貨店にブティックなどが集まるショッピングコンプレックス
diverse 多様な、様々の
recommend...ing …することを勧める　recommend to choose とは言えません
cool いいね、OK だ、すばらしい
　　ex. How about next Saturday? Cool!　来週の土曜日はどう。いいよ。

本文中で使われている単語を用いて英文を完成させましょう。

1. 当店ではワインを多数取りそろえております。

   [   ] [   ] a wide selection of wines.

2. 喜んで町をご案内します。

   I'm very [   ] to show you around the town.

3. それを買うことをお薦めします。

   I [   ] [   ] that.

4. 私はかまわないわよ。

   That's [   ] ([   ] [   ]) with me.

5. 僕はなんと言ってもタイガースファンだ。

   I am [   ] a Tigers fan.

6. 他に何かできますか。

   What [   ] can you do?

7. その新しい髪型とってもいいね。

   You look pretty [   ] with that new haircut.

8. しり込みしないで (遠慮しないで、恥ずかしがらないで)。

   Don't be [   ].

9. クイーン・ストリートはオークランド一の繁華街です。

   Queen Street is the [   ] street in Auckland.

10. 僕の父は多趣味です。

    My father's interests are very [   ].

異 文 化 理 解

ここに登場してくれた① Katie (クライストチャーチ出身 若い女性)、② Chris (オークランド出身 中華系 男性)、③ Mabel (クリスの母親)、④ Joel (オークランド出身 若い男性) のそれぞれのメッセージにおいて共通して語られていたポイント (共通して使われていた単語・語句) をピックアップしてみましょう。そして彼らのトークから、オークランドについてどのような印象を受けたか話し合ってみましょう。

Unit 7

Local people in Auckland (2)

この Unit では、オークランド市中心部の対岸に位置するデボンポートのヴィクトリア・ストリート (Victoria Street) 沿いにある古書店ブックマーク (BookMark)、宝飾・雑貨店トティ (TOTI)、ニュージーランド土産店グリーン・プラネット (Green Planet) で働く人たちから、これからニュージーランドで英語を勉強する日本人学生へのメッセージをもらいました。TOTI で働くブリムリー (Brimley) はイギリス生まれですが、BookMark で働くマーティン (Martin) と Green Planet でアルバイトをしているオークランド大学生のホリー (Holy) はニュージーランド生まれのニュージーランド育ちです。そして最後は、オークランドの目抜き通りクイーン・ストリートにあるプラティパス (Platypus) という靴屋さんで、店員エビータ (Evita) が語ってくれた「外国人からみた日本の寿司」についての話を聞いてみましょう。

7-1 スカイタワーから見たデボンポート

まずはデボンポートの紹介です。

> A short ferry ride from Auckland's CBD, Devonport is a heritage and arts destination; a seaside village to explore...

Dating from the mid 1800s Devonport is one of Auckland's most historically authentic villages. It's a place where time slows down, where boutique shops fill the spaces of Victorian-era buildings, and dining is always a relaxed and enjoyable experience. With some of the best beaches in the city, the golden sands and calm blue waters are right on our doorsteps. We welcome you to our piece of paradise.　　(Devonport [https://www.devonport.co.nz/] のトップページより引用)

まさに "piece of paradise" そのもののビーチ

Words & Phrases

CBD Unit 1 の p. 5 の Words & Phrases を参照
Dating from date from= (起源が) …にさかのぼる、…から始まる
boutique ［形容詞］少数の顧客に良質の製品やサービスを提供する
　　ex. boutique hotel 小規模高級ホテル
right ［副詞］まさしく、ちょうど
　　ex. I'm right behind you. 私はあなたの真後ろにいる (あなたを絶対支持する)。
piece of paradise 小さな楽園　piece (土地の) 小区画

Martin@BookMark

🎧 25 Martin@BookMark

(So some comments for students, please!)

OK. Well…hello, Akira and Shinako. It's very nice to see you both in our book-shop today; I'm Martin; I work at BookMark in Devonport and we'd love people to come in from whatever country who are interested in books and we'd make them welcome in our shop and so I hope that some of your lovely students will also come in and see us at some stage. Very nice to meet you both.

Words & Phrases

BookMark ブックマーク (店名)　元来の意味は「本のしおり」
whatever (名詞の前に置いて) どんな…でも
　　ex. I want a box, whatever size is fine.　どんな大きさでもいい、箱がほしい。
make them welcome make…welcome ＝…を温かく迎える
lovely すばらしい、美しい　以前の Unit では "lovely" という語は女性が使っていましたが、ここでは男性が使っています。"lovely" は「主に女性が用いる」という表記を付けている英和辞典もありますが、男性が使ってもおかしくないということです。
at some stage いつか　stage ＝時期　ex. at one stage　あるとき

ヴィクトリア・ストリート沿いの The Arcade とその中に入っている BookMark

26 Brimley@TOTI

("Hello, Brimley!"- "Hello, Shinako!"- "Please!")

I love living in New Zealand, I love living in Auckland. I think our scenery is beautiful, our beaches are stunning, the people...the people are warm and friendly. But I think, most of all, I think New Zealand is safe; it is a safe country to live in. I love living here and I hope if your students come they will love living here too. (Thank you!)

Words & Phrases

I love living here love doing something は〈イギリス英語〉
cf. love to do something〈アメリカ英語〉 I love to live here. Unit 3 の p.14 の Words & Phrases を参照

stunning ひじょうに美しい、すばらしい cf. stun …を気絶（ぼうっと）させる

TOTI が入っているヴィクトリア・ストリート沿いの Devonia Building（左）とデボンポートの入り口に立つ 1903 年創業の The Esplanade Hotel

 7-2 A "stunning" beach　映像の中で聞こえるのはセミの鳴き声です。

 7-3 ニュージーランドのセミ　興味のある方はぜひ

🎧 27 ▸ **Holly@Green Planet**

(So, could you give some advice for Japanese students?) Um, my name's Holly...and...yeah, I would say to any Japanese students wanting to come and study in New Zealand, that it's a great opportunity. Um...there's several universities that have awesome culture and...um...education offered at them, and an opportunity to study overseas is awesome because it's such a friendly, warm and welcoming community over here.

Words & Phrases

awesome すごい、すてきな、恐ろしい、すさまじい

🎧 28 ▸ **Evita@Platypus**

(I wish you will have a great time in Tokyo next year!) I know I'm so excited; I just wanna try the food; like all the different kinds of food. (Ah, yes) It's so interesting (Sushi in Japan, it's quite different) I hear, yeah, that's what um my friend; he went with er..his girlfriend to Japan and he was like... you know, he's from England (oh, yes) so he went, and they wanted to order sushi, and it was like "Live or not alive?", he was like "alive, what do you mean, alive?" and it was like, you know, like tentacles and (yes) a lot of live seafood; Kinda like that (ah, you do?) yeah (oh, that's perfect! some people find it a bit hard to enjoy raw stuff but it, it should be...um...it's all safe...) yeah, and it's better for your body (hum, I think so and the good combination of local vegetables and such a fish is very healthy) yeah, yeah, it's really really good for your insides (yeah they are so popular...)

Words & Phrases

that's what my friend 次に "said" くらいを補ってみる

like Unit 5 の p. 22 の Words & Phrases を参照

he is from England...so he went イングランド（イギリス）は首都ロンドンをはじめ至る所にすし屋（その大半はテイクアウェイ専門店か回転ずし店）があるので、ある意味イングランド（イギリス）人は「すし通」と言えます。だから「彼は日本のすし屋に行った」。

Live or not alive? 正確には Alive or not alive? 日本のすし屋初体験の彼が、眼の前に現れたすし（のネタ）を見ての第一印象がこれ。

tentacles （タコの）触手、つまり「タコの足」のこと

Kinda =kind of いくらか、多少、やや ex. It's kinda cold, isn't it? ちょっと寒いですね。

insides お腹 ex. I have something wrong with my insides. お腹の調子がよくない。

本文中で使われている単語を用いて英文を完成させましょう。

1. とっても楽しかったです。

   We've had a [　　　　　　] time.

2. どんな本でも好きなものを読んでよろしい。

   You may read [　　　　　　] book you like.

3. ウァー、それすごくいいね。
   Wow! That's totally [　　　　　　].

4. 彼は美しい声をしている。
   He has a [　　　　　　] voice.

5. ここから湖の絶景がご覧になれます。

   You can get a [　　　　　　] view of the lake from here.

6. 僕の父はサッカー観戦が好きだ。

   My dad [　　　　　　] going to see football games.

7. 大学への往復はバスでかなり時間がかかる。

   It's a long bus [　　　　　　] to and from the university.

8. バスはまさに時間通りにやってきた。

   The bus arrived [　　　　　　] on time.

9. 日本にお迎えできて何よりです。

   It is my pleasure to [　　　　　　] you to Japan.

10. それは君が前に言ったことと違う。

    That's not [　　　　　　] you said before.

異文化理解

ニュージーランドにも sushi がすっかり定着しています。フードコードにも sushi 店が入り、ランチに sushi を買って公園などで楽しむ姿もすっかりおなじみです。人気のチェーン店では、パーティ用の sushi のケータリングサービスも展開していますし（下の写真）、和食レストランでのディナーにおいても sushi は定番です。

人気 sushi チェーン店によるケータリングサービス

＊写真の sushi を見て気づいたことを話し合ってみましょう（巻頭のカラー写真も参照）。

お洒落な和食レストランでのディナーにおいても sushi
は定番メニューのひとつ

＊写真はアボカド・ロール sushi ですが、気づいたことを話し合ってみましょう。

こういった背景もあり、ニュージーランドにおいても「好きなたべものは sushi！」という人が少なくないのですが、ここに登場してくれた Evita のトークを聞いていると、実際に日本を旅した彼女の友人たちが体験した sushi は、彼らが普段楽しんでいるニュージーランドの sushi とはひとあじ違ったようですね。ニュージーランドで親しまれている sushi と、日本の sushi はどこが共通していて、どこが異なっていると思いますか。また、日本にも、海外からとりいれられてすっかり定着した料理がたくさんありますが、その代表的なものをあげ、現地とはどこがどのように違っているかについて話し合ってみましょう。

Reading newspapers (1)

この Unit では、現地の新聞ニュージーランド・ヘラルド (The New Zealand Herald) を通じて、ニュージーランドの文化を学びましょう。今回の記事の舞台は、ニュージーランド北島にあるヘースティングズという街にある、マクドナルドのお店です。マクドナルドと言えば、アメリカ発祥の世界規模で展開するファストフード店で、世界のどこに行ってもほぼ画一、均一化された商品が提供されるのが大前提です。ところが、そんなお店の中で突然、ニュージーランドのマオリの文化が主張を始めることになります。さてそのきっかけをつくったのは…。

Big Mac, te reo with that?

Video of Maori language exchange at McDonald's store in Hawke's Bay goes viral

The New Zealand Herald | Thursday, September 7, 2017   Sarah Harris

A McDonald's store has become the unlikely platform for Maori language revival after a video of a woman ordering in te reo, and being responded to in kind, went viral.

Hastings McDonald's worker Jershon Tatana, 17, surprised the group of Maori-language enthusiasts when he spoke their language back to them.

The video, taken by language advocate Jeremy Tatere McLeod, has had more than 70,000 views.

McLeod had organised a breakfast at McDonald's for te reo speakers in an effort to normalise Maori language. Holding regular social events was one of the goals from the Ngati Kahungunu Iwi Inc symposium.

McLeod said they had phoned ahead and told McDonald's that they were coming in but they didn't expect them to have staff who knew te reo.

"He started speaking back - we were absolutely blown away. We were very pleasantly surprised."

McLeod said the new environment forced students to learn and create new words for the situation.

"We need to make the language relevant to our children. If they don't see any relevance why would they bother learning it? He [Tatana] is an outstanding role model for young people and the future of our language rests with his generation."

Tatana wasn't able to speak to the *Herald* as he's in the middle of a regional basketball tournament, but his mum Learna Karena said he was overwhelmed by the attention.

Neither Karena or Tatana's dad were fluent in te reo but Tatana had been in Maori immersion learning for his early childhood and primary school years and was passionate about the language. He now goes to St Johns College and does one hour of Maori language a week.

"It comes natural to him. He can think in Maori and English."

"When he had 20 people coming up to him to order their kai he didn't have to think."

Give it a go

● To order a Big Mac and fries in te reo, try this: Ka taea e au he Big Mac me ngā riwai parai koa. (Can I have a Big Mac and fries please)

Words & Phrases

Big Mac, te reo with that?
　　te reo　マオリ語 (Maori = the language)
　　with that　それ (ビッグ・マック) と一緒に　Unit 4 の p. 17 の Words & Phrases を参照
　　cf.　Customer: Can I have a Big Mac, please? ビッグ・マックをください。
　　　　　　Clerk: Sure. Would you like a drink and fries with that?　はい。一緒に飲み物とポテトは
　　　　　　　　いかがですか。
goes viral　(インターネットなどで) 一気に広まる
　　go =(ある状態に) なる　ex. Eggs soon go bad in hot weather. 卵は暑いとすぐに悪くなる(腐る)。
　　viral =ウィルスの、(インターネット経由で) 急速に広まる、人気が出る
　　〈語法・文法〉新聞の見出しは、過去形 (一気に広まった) は現在形 (一気に広まる) で代用されま
　　す。一方記事の本文 2 行目は went viral と過去形になっています。また Video of Maori language
　　exchange のように Video の前の冠詞 (A / The) が見出しでは省略されています。一方記事の本文
　　2 行目は a video と冠詞がついています。
in kind　同じ種類のもので (マオリ語で)
　　ex. I replied to her insult in kind.　彼女の無礼には私も無礼で答えた。
Hastings　ヘースティングズ (ニュージーランド北東部の都市) 人口約 7 万人
speak...back　(マオリ語で) 話し返す　back = [副詞] (…) し返す
　　cf. I'll call you back later. 後で折り返しお電話します。
language advocate　マオリ語支持 (擁護) 者
organise　〈イギリス英語〉…を企画する　= organize
normalise　〈イギリス英語〉…を標準化する　= normalize
Ngati Kahungunu Iwi Inc　ンガティ・カフングヌ部族法人
　　Iwi = (マオリ語) 部族、種族　Inc = incorporated =法人 (会社) 組織の
ahead　あらかじめ
they were coming in　これからそちらへ行く=これから電話を受けている (聞いている) マクドナル
　　ドの店へ行く
　　〈語法・文法〉「相手 (聞き手) の方へ行く」場合は go ではなく come になります。
　　例えば電話で Akira と Ken が話をしていて、「Akira が Ken の主催する (あるいは Ken も出席する)

パーティーに行く」ことを Ken（＝電話の話し相手、聞き手）に伝える場合は、Akira は Ken に "I'm coming to the party." と言わなければなりません。"I'm going to the party." だと、聞き手の Ken とは全く関係のないパーティーに行くことになります。

blown away　びっくりした、感動した
　　blow away ＝…をびっくりさせる、感動させる、…を吹き散らす、吹き飛ばす
relevant　実際的（社会的）に意味のある、（当面の問題と）密接に関連がある
bother　（普通は否定文、疑問文で）わざわざ…する
　　ex. I'll get you a tea? Oh, please don't bother.　お茶をお持ちしましょうか。いえ、おかまいなく。
role model　理想の姿
rest with　…次第だ　ex. The decision rests with him. 決定は彼次第だ。
immersion learning　没入学習　ここでは、マオリ語のみを使ってマオリ語を学習すること
primary school　初等学校（1 年生〜 8 年生＝ 5 歳〜 12 歳）
St John's College　ヘースティングズにある男子生徒が通うカトリック系の半官半民 (state-integrated) の中等学校（9 年生〜 13 年生＝ 13 歳〜 19 歳）
　　※ニュージーランドの教育制度については https://parents.education.govt.nz を参照
does　do ＝（学課を）勉強する、専攻する
　　ex. My son does two hours of British literature classes a week.　息子は週 2 時間英文学の授業を受けている（勉強をしている）。
kai　（マオリ語）食べ物
give it a go　いっちょうやってみる　go ＝ [名詞] やってみること、ひと試み

EXCERCISES　空所補充

本文中で使われている単語を用いて英文を完成させましょう。

1. あの写真はネット上で一気に広まった。

　　That picture went [　　　　　　　] on the Internet.

2. 後で折り返しお電話します。

　　I'll call you [　　　　　　] later.

3. 次は前もって電話してください。

　　Next time phone [　　　　　　].

4. すぐそちらに行きます。

　　I'm [　　　　　　].

5. わざわざ待ってくれなくっていいよ。

　　Don't [　　　　　　] waiting for me.

次の1～5の英文が正しければ（　　　）内にTを、間違っていればFを入れましょう。

1. （　　　）

   A McDonald's store has become the platform for Maori language revival because the group of Maori-language enthusiasts have their meeting at a McDonald's every week.

2. （　　　）

   McLeod had organised a breakfast at McDonald's for te reo speakers mainly because one of their goals was to normalise Maori language in daily social events.

3. （　　　）

   McLeod did not expect to be talked to in te reo, although she had called ahead and let McDonald's know that they were coming.

4. （　　　）

   Tatana became fluent in te reo thanks to his parents who were both fluent in the Maori language.

5. （　　　）

   Tatana could not speak to the *Herald* because he was too shy to do that.

異 文 化 理 解

本記事では、Tatana くんは、同世代の若者のよきロールモデルであると記されています。彼の行為は、彼と同世代のニュージーランドの若者に具体的にどのような影響を与えると思いますか。また、マオリ語・マオリ文化の保護・普及をめざして、ニュージーランドでは具体的にどのような取り組みがなされているか、調べてみましょう。

Unit 9
Maori-culture and multi-culture

Unit 8ではマクドナルドでのマオリ語による会話が話題になっていました。この Unit では、5歳の時に中国から移住してきた20代女性アン（Ann）へのインタビューを通して、中国人でありかつキウイ（ニュージーランド人）であるというアイデンティティを持つ彼女から見た「多文化主義国家ニュージーランド」の現状を学びましょう。

 9-1 様々な人種が行き交うスクランブル交差点

Ann (China & Kiwi)

29 Ann

(So, hi, Ann! (huhu...Kia Ora!) Do you have any advice or message for the young Japanese students who are very much interested in studying in New Zealand, especially in Auckland?)

Especially in Auckland...um...woo! (laugh). For Japanese students that are coming in to Auckland, I recommend you to get to know everything about the culture, everything about Maori-culture and also the Kiwi culture because it's important to be more open-minded, and...er...to just talk to people and learn more about other people's perspectives and their ways as well as your own, as well as your...share your own story as well because through that you learn more about yourself...you explore more of your identity, but most importantly, you learn more about other people and also, I would say definitely, definitely learn about Maori-culture because that is so important in Auckland 'cause...um...you learn that...er...the history tells you about the land, the spirit, it tells you about...um... just how New Zealand came to be and how...like just Maori people value this land so much...and...and...I don't know what else to say...but how do I explain it like...er...let me just think...um...(pause)

Words & Phrases

Kia Ora! マオリ語　Hello! Hi!
Kiwi culture ニュージーランド文化　先住民マオリ族の文化とイギリス文化とが融合して形成されたもの
share your own story　with other people を補ってみる。 share ＝…を話す、分かち合う
　ex. Please share the secret with us. その秘密を我々に話してください。

through that そうすることで　through ＝…によって、…のおかげで
　ex. You can only achieve success through hard work.　一生懸命働いてはじめて成功をつかむことができる。

came to be 今のようになった
　cf. How did you come to be a doctor?　どうして君は医者になったの。

let me just think ちょっと考えさせて

Devonport Library の時間外返却口（マオリ語との2か国語表記）

 9-2 電車の車内アナウンスもマオリ語との2か国語で

 Ann

You want to...um...you will find that there's a lot of Aucklanders that probably don't know Maori-culture as much...um...but that's because they've lived here all, all their lives and so they're used to, they're used to being bombarded by their cultural...um...cultural history, but if you are here, and if you are able to gain that Maori-knowledge and the Kiwi knowledge, then you are one step ahead of Aucklanders but also you get to...um just how do I...just experience the spirit of...of um...er...yeah that's a lot of the Maori-culture...(yes) oh I don't know...

Words & Phrases

they're used to being bombarded 攻撃される（攻め立てられる）のに慣れている
　ex. We have been bombarded with letters of complaint.　苦情の投書に攻め立てられている。

cultural history マオリ文化とイギリス文化とが融合してきた歴史

ahead of …にまさって、…より進んで
　ex. She's far ahead of me in English. 彼女は僕よりはるかに英語がよくできる。
　cf. Tokyo is three hours behind Auckland.　東京はオークランドより3時間遅れている。

how do I say または explain くらいを補ってみる。

31 Ann

(Yes! That's good! and um you mentioned identity (yes), your story (yes), so could you please tell us a bit about your own story? your roots or...)

My own story? OK... my own story is that I am a Chinese who came here when I was five years old and I was brought up in New Zealand. Um...my identity is being a Kiwi and being a Chinese. Sometimes it's very hard because I try to preserve my traditional customs, traditional roots, but the same time...um...there're often...Kiwi culture tries to um...make, like, er...what's the word...I'm often like pressured to conform to Kiwi culture and sometimes you can feel a bit left out...um...because Kiwi people don't know your roots and they don't...they look at you and they're like "Ah, I don't understand!" but it's totally OK because you will have to find the people who, um who are also Asian, who are also Kiwi, and then you just find your own family and your own friends.

Words & Phrases

what's the word (?) (前の make に続けることばが出てこなくて) 何て言ったらいいか
※結局 make に続けることばが出てこなかったので、違う表現に切り替えています。

I'm often like pressured to... (to... 以下しなければいけないという) プレッシャーを受けることがよくある

feel left out 疎外感を味わう
ex. I felt left out at the party because no one spoke to me. 誰もパーティーで話しかけてくれなかったので、疎外感を味わった。

"Ah, I don't understand!" (中国人に見えるあなたが自分たちと同じように話せることに気づき)
「わあ、どういうこと！」といった驚いたような、意外なような顔つきをすること

totally 全く、全然、すっかり　ex. This is totally different from that.　これとそれとは全く違う。

32 Ann

(Good! Thank you very much and last question, what are you majoring...um...at your university and what is your future goal?)

I'm majoring in Digital Media and Communication Studies. Um, I don't know what I want to do yet, but that's OK! I'm still discovering every day. I'm 21 years old (yes!), I actually don't know what I wanna do at all, but I'm just focusing on what I love doing, which is dancing...um...which is meeting people, which is...um...just...um...being patient with myself, being kind to myself...and my future goal is to travel around the world and meet different people. (Wonderful! Sounds great! Thank you very much, Ann!) That's OK!

Words & Phrases

EXCERCISES 空所補充

本文中で使われている単語を用いて英文を完成させましょう。

1. それは名案のようだ。

   That [   ] (like) a good idea.

2. 現在ニュージーランドは日本より 3 時間進んでいる。

   Currently New Zealand is three hours [   ] of Japan.

3. 僕が就職できたのは叔父のおかげだ。

   It was [   ] my uncle that I got the job.

4. 議論は 2 つの主要な問題に集中した。

   The discussion [   ] on two main problems.

5. ねえ、僕にやらせてください。

   Here, [   ] me do it.

6. 我々はお互い何でも話すから二人の間に秘密はない。

   We [   ] everything—we have no secrets.

7. ここには日本語で話せる友だちがひとりもいない。

   I have no friends to talk [   ] in Japanese.

8. ロンドンは東京より 9 時間遅れている。

   London is nine hours [   ] Tokyo.

9. まったく同感です。

   I [   ] agree with you.

10. 右側運転にはまだ慣れていません。

I'm not [   ] to driving on the right.

①私たちがニュージーランドのような多文化主義国家で学ぶ・暮らすことにはどのような意味があると
思いますか。私たちはどのようなことを学ぶことができるでしょうか。また、どのような困難に直面
することが予想されますか。ペア、もしくは 3 ～ 4 人のグループをつくり、自由に討論してみましょう。

②この Unit で自らの生い立ちについて話してくれた Ann は、英語と中国語の両方を自由に話すこと
ができる二重言語使用者 (いわゆる、バイリンガル) です。日本では、2 つ以上の言語を自由に使
いこなすことができる人の数はまだそれほど多くはなく、「バイリンガル」は憧れだと感じる人もいる
でしょう。一方、Ann は、複数の言語をつかい、複数の文化的背景をもっていることには非常に難
しい面があることを率直に語っています。ペア、もしくは 3 ～ 4 人のグループをつくり、bilingual で
あること、bicultural であることについて思うことを自由に議論してみましょう。その際には、功罪、
光と影の両面からこの問題について考察すること、意見を述べる際には、なぜそう思うのか、その
理由についてもきちんとことばにして述べることを特に意識してみましょう。

①と②については、日本語、もしくは英語で討論してみましょう。

Reading newspapers (2)

この Unit では、多文化主義国家ニュージーランドにおける移民を取り上げます。アメリカでもヨーロッパでも、移民問題は避けては通れないものになり、記事本文にもあるように、移民問題はいまや政治問題になっていると言っても過言ではありません。移民が増えることで様々な問題が生じていることは事実です。この記事やUnit 9 のアンの話は、多文化主義と移民問題は相容れないものなのかどうかという問題を提起しています。

Immigrants understated by 60,000

The New Zealand Herald | Tuesday, September 5, 2017

The number of net migrants coming into the country since 2001 has been underestimated by nearly 60,000, Statistics New Zealand says.

The Government's statistics department has confirmed that a new measure to more closely check patterns of migration has revealed a problem in the older method.

Last year a measure was brought in to track actual travel histories, whereas previous statistics were based on what people said they would do on their arrival cards.

While the card-based system showed 300,000 extra people had moved to New Zealand since 2001, the real figure was probably about 59,000—or nearly 20 per cent—higher, Statistics NZ has confirmed.

Of that figure, 45,000 arrived in 2001 and 2002.

NZ First leader Winston Peters, whose party has promised to slash immigration, said the Government had explaining to do.

"Minister of Immigration Michael Woodhouse should have been asking questions when NZ First kept pointing out the country is being overwhelmed by migrants," he said.

"Statistics NZ have been nothing but amateur sleuths using an outdated method that relies on people sticking to plans, and their honesty."

New Zealand has been experiencing record levels of net migration in recent years, with rising immigration a key election issue as it strains infrastructure and is blamed for inflating property markets.

Net migration rose to a new record for the year to July, according to Statistics NZ, reaching 72,400.

Words & Phrases

Immigrants understated 〈語法・文法〉新聞の見出しでは、受け身の場合 be 動詞が省略されます。一方記事本文の 1 ～ 2 行目は The number...has been underestimated となっています。
understate ＝（数など）を実際より少なめに言う

by 60,000 6 万人程度（まで） by ＝…の程度まで、（ある数値）だけ
ex. Prices have risen by 10 per cent. 物価は 1 割上がった。

net 正味の、最終的な

Statistics New Zealand ニュージーランド統計局

statistics department 統計局

measure ［普通は複数形で］手段、方法 ex. measures against illegal immigration 不法入国対策

pattern （行動などの）型

track …を（痕跡・証拠などをたどって）突き止める

travel histories 渡航歴

arrival card ニュージーランド入国審査カード

card-based system 入国審査カードに基づく（移民の数を把握する）方法

figure 数字、数値 ex. unemployment figures 失業者数

Of that figure その数字のうちの

NZ First New Zealand First ＝ニュージーランド・ファースト党

party 政党、党 ex. a ruling party 与党 an opposition party 野党

slash …を大幅に削減する

explaining 説明、釈明
ex. The prime minister has a lot of explaining to do. 首相には釈明する余地が大いにある。

Minister of Immigration 移民大臣

nothing but …に過ぎない、全く…だ

amateur sleuth 素人探偵

people sticking to plans 人々が（入国審査カードに記入した）計画を守ること
stick to ＝…を守る、…に忠実である
ex. Once you make a decision, you must stick to it. いったん決めたら、それを守りなさい。

record levels 記録的な水準

a key election issue 選挙の主たる争点
issue ＝争点、問題点 ex. a political issue 政治問題

strain …を逼迫させる

infrastructure インフラ（ストラクチャー）＝水道・電気・鉄道・学校・工場などの文明社会の基本設備

inflate （物価）をつり上げる

property market 不動産市場

for the year to July 今年（の初めから）7 月までの間に

本文中で使われている単語を用いて英文を完成させましょう。

1. テロ防止のためにはより思い切った対策が必要とされた。

   More drastic [   ] were required to prevent terrorism.

2. その補助金はもめごとの種にしかなっていない。

   The subsidies have been [   ] [   ] trouble.

3. インターネットが犯罪の増加を招いたと非難されている。

   The Internet has been [   ] for the increase in crime.

4. 彼の話は必ず脱線する。

   He never [   ] to the point.

5. 売り上げは10パーセント上昇している。

   Sales are up [   ] 10 %.

EXCERCISES T or F

次の1～5の英文が正しければ(   )内にTを、間違っていればFを入れましょう。

1. (   )

   The real number of immigrants coming into New Zealand since 2001 is about 300,000.

2. (   )

   "Of that figure" means exactly "Of 359,000."

3. (   )

   This article says NZ First has explaining to do for slashing immigration.

4. (   )

   People do not always say what they would do on the arrival cards.

5. (   )

   The Minister of Immigration listened to NZ First when they were pointing out the problem rising migrants might cause.

Reading newspapers (3)

この Unit では、タトゥー（入れ墨）を取り上げます。日本での（日本人の）タトゥーに対するイメージと、ニュージーランドでの（キウイの）タトゥーに対するイメージとは大きな隔たりがあるといえるでしょう。ニュージーランドを代表する映画俳優のサム・ニールさんは、ある意味「思いつき」でタトゥーを入れることにしました。しかし彼の「思いつき」の背後には大変重要な意味づけがなされていることに注目しましょう。

Sam Neill gets his mark of respect

Herald on Sunday, September 2, 2018 Lee Umbers

Blockbusting new documentary series *Uncharted* with Sam Neill explores the mark Captain James Cook left on New Zealand and the Pacific.

And being at the helm of the show has left its mark on Neill too, with his first tattoo at the age of 69.

Neill got ink on his forearm from ta moko artist Gordon Toi during filming last year.

Toi, a friend of Neill's since they both acted in 1993 Academy Award-winning Kiwi drama *The Piano*, said they were chatting about their past between takes at his then Mangere Bridge-based House of Natives studio.

He was preparing to tattoo his daughter Wairingiringi, 22, for the next scene when Neill said "actually would I mind if I did a piece on him".

"The whole place just went quiet," Toi said. "That...not only blew me away but blew the crew away as well."

"It definitely wasn't in the script."

Neill told the *Herald on Sunday* his decision "was a bit of a spur of the moment but I thought, Gordon's the man".

His reason for wanting the tattoo had "to do with connecting myself to [my] country".

Neill entrusted Toi, who has been at the forefront of a ta moko revival, with designing his piece.

"I said...you'll know [the appropriate design]. You know me. He said, I do know you and I'll do what I think you need."

Toi, of Ngāti Wharara, said during filming for the *Uncharted* episode he and

Neill had been discussing the significance of the spiral symbol in Polynesian culture.

It was used to represent a person's path in life and the powerful convergence of energies from that course, he said.

Toi thought it was "appropriate that I tattoo that on him".

Neill's piece represented "his journey in life and the connection between him and my family, and his own family".

It was apt for *Uncharted*, which followed Captain Cook's historic journey.

Toi said Neill was "solid" throughout the tattooing, which was watched by the actor's son, Tim.

"It wasn't a big piece but it was a significant piece. We were all pretty close to tears by the time the thing was finished," Toi said.

Neill was "delighted" with his piece and grateful to Toi.

"It's extremely personal to me, and I wouldn't have wanted anyone else but Gordon to do it." The tattoo made him "feel strangely perhaps more connected" to Aotearoa.

Words & Phrases

Some Neill　サム・ニール（北アイルランド生まれのニュージーランドの映画俳優）

blockbusting　大ヒットの

Uncharted with Sam Neill　ジェームズ・クック（Captain James Cook [1728-79]）の第 1 回航海（1768-71）から 250 年となる 2018 年、俳優のサム・ニールがクックの足跡を追って旅をするニュージーランドのプライムテレビ制作のテレビ番組　uncharted ＝海図にない

at the helm　…の舵（＝指揮）をとって

got ink on his forearm　＝got his forearm inked　前腕にタトゥーを入れてもらった
　　cf. I must get my hair cut. 髪を切ってもらわないといけない。
　　※ちなみにこの記事の電子版では "Neill received a piece on his forearm" と修正されています。

ta moko　Maori tattoo

Gordon Toi　ゴードン・トイ

The Piano　日本公開時のタイトルは『ピアノ・レッスン』

take　（映画などの）ワンシーンの撮影

then　その時の、当時の　ex. the then conditions　その当時の状況

Mangere Bridge　マンゲレ・ブリッジ　オークランド中心部から見て南西に位置する郊外の地区

Wairingiringi　ワイリンギリンギ

piece　（タトゥー）1 作品

went　Unit 8 の p.39 の Words & Phrases を参照

blow away　Unit 8 の p.40 の Words & Phrases を参照

script　（*Uncharted* の）台本、脚本

a spur of the moment　できごころ、時のはずみ

man　（…に）ふさわしい男、適任者

had to do with　have to do with ＝…と関係がある
　　ex. Did you have anything to do with that plan? あの計画になにか関わっていましたか。

Ngāti Wharara　ワララ部族　ngāti ＝（マオリ語）部族

spiral symbol 渦巻き型 (koru) の象徴

convergence 一点に集まること
close to tears 今にも泣きそう　close to ＝もう少しで…しそうである、ほとんど…
　　ex. The report is close to completion.　報告書はほとんど出来上がってる。
but …以外に、…を除いて
　　ex. Everyone but Akira is here. アキラ以外はみんなここにいる。
　　cf. It is nothing but a joke. それは冗談以外の何ものでもない。それはほんの冗談だ。
Aotearoa ニュージーランドのマオリ語名「長く白い雲の地」という意味

EXCERCISES　空所補充

本文中で使われている単語を用いて英文を完成させましょう。

1. 彼はもう少しで秘密を打ち明けてしまいそうだった。

   He was [　　　　　　] [　　　　　　　] confessing the secret.

2. 一人を除いて全員が死亡した。

   All [　　　　　　] one died.

3. 写真を撮ってもらえませんか。もちろんいいですよ。

   Would you [　　　　　] taking our picture? Of course [　　　　　].

4. 彼はこの計画に大きく関わっている。

   He has a lot to do [　　　　] this project.

5. 彼は怒って真っ赤になった。

   He [　　　　　] red with anger.

次の1〜5の英文が正しければ（　　　）内にTを、間違っていればFを入れましょう。

1. （　　　）

Sam Neill got his forearm inked and it was his second tattoo in his life.

2. （　　　）

The crew of the documentary series *Uncharted* had been expecting that Neill would wish to get inked because of Toi's influence.

3. （　　　）

Neill said that the idea of getting tattooed had just occurred to him without thinking about it much.

4. （　　　）

Neill had not known the meaning of the spiral symbol until he had it on his forearm.

5. （　　　）

Neill's son Tim could not bear to see his father's tattooing because he thought it was too scary.

異文化理解

> サム・ニールさんの記事を読んで（＝サム・ニールさんの前腕に彫られたタトゥーの意味を知って）、タトゥーに対するみなさんの考えはどう変わりましたか。またラグビーワールドカップ2019日本大会の開催に先立ち、ラグビーの国際統括団体ワールドラグビー (WR) は、出場する選手にタトゥーを隠すよう要請する方針です。また事前にこのことを打診された各国のチームからは苛立ちの反応があるものと思われていましたが、そのような反応はないとのことです。ニュージーランドのメディアによると、同国協会幹部は「どの遠征に行くときも私たちは地元文化を尊重する。それは来年日本に行く時も何ら変わらない」と、WRの方針に賛成する意思を示したとのこと (SANSPO.COM 2018年9月21日)。みなさんはこの各国の対応、とりわけニュージーランドの対応をどのように考えますか。

Unit 12

On the streets of Auckland

最後の Unit では、オークランド市内を散策しながら目に留まった看板やポスターなどを紹介します。面白いもの、気の利いたもの、いかにもニュージーランドらしいものなど、様々な看板とそこに書かれている英語を楽しみましょう。看板の英語が読めない（＝理解できない）ようではその町の暮らしに溶け込むことはできません。言い換えれば、看板の英語が理解できて初めてその土地で生活できると言っても過言ではありません。

On Ponsonby Road

When I was walking on Ponsonby Road, along which many cafes, restaurants, nightclubs, art galleries and upmarket shops are located, the signboard of a second-hand bookstore caught my eye.

The signboard said 'Not all those who wander are lost.' —Tolkien So wander in

Just as Tolkien put it, I was wandering, though I was not lost.

Anyway, I wandered in to the bookstore, The Open Book, following the direction of the signboard to the letter.

At the entrance were two chairs. →

A small piece of paper with an arrow pointing to the chairs below said **Take a seat. Literally. Free!**

I visited The Open Book again one week later to find one of the two chairs had gone!

Someone must have taken it home *literally*.

1. What does "Take a seat" usually mean?
2. What does "Take a seat" on the small paper mean?

Words & Phrases

Not all those who wander are lost. この 1 行はイギリスの児童文学者・中世英文学研究者である Tolkien (1892-1973) の代表作 *The Lord of the Rings* (『指輪物語』) の中に出てくる *"All That Is Gold Does Not Glitter"* という詩の一節。"Not all those who wander are lost." も *"All that is gold does not glitter"* もいずれも部分否定になっていることに注意しましょう。

ex. Not all the members were present. メンバーの全員が出席したわけではない。

wander in …に迷い込む、…へぶらぶらと入っていく

to the letter 文字通りに、厳密に

ex. They carried out my instructions to the letter. 彼らは私の指示を文字通りに果たした。

as Tolkien put it トールキンが言ったように

as...put it …が言ったように put =…を言い表す、言う

ex. As Shakespeare put it, brevity is the soul of wit.
シェイクスピアが言ったように、簡潔は知恵の精髄だ。

On Victoria Street in Devonport

I was walking along Victoria Street when I happened to find a very nice secondhand bookshop, BookMark. Inside, a very large poster caught my eye.

The poster said **There is no App / To replace your Lap! Read to your child.**

In front of the entrance a small picture was leaning against the wall.
A dog in the picture is asking passersby to take his owner out of BookMark;
"Can you please tell my owner it's raining again and I'm wet and cold and he's been in Bookmark for ages!" In fact, BookMark stocks such an ample selection of quality secondhand and rare books that we cannot help losing ourselves in the world of books.

Words & Phrases

App =application　アプリケーション　ここではパソコン、スマホくらいの意味　Lap と韻を踏んでいます。

Bottomless Lunch $ 50
2 Hour Package
Bookings essential!
-Sharing entrée
-Choice of main
-Sharing sides
-Bottomless* mimosa,
 estrella, prosecco or
 mocktails / soft drinks
Every Saturday 12-4
 *Ts & Cs apply

Words & Phrases

entrée 前菜
mimosa ミモサ (カクテル)
estrella スペイン、バルセロナのビール

prosecco プロセッコ (スパークリングワイン)
mocktail ノンアルコールカクテル
Ts & Cs = terms and conditions

Today's Special: Order two drinks and pay for both ☺
—I know that without being told!

Why limit HAPPY HOUR to one hour?
HAPPY HOUR from 3-7 pm!
—Oh, you are very generous!

「当店では未成年者へのアルコールの提供を固くお断りさせて頂いております。」

In NZ, the warning is very brief and very strict!
Translate what the notice says into a catchy Japanese phrase.

A Reminder to All In NZ, daylight saving ends each year at 3 am on the first Sunday of April (and starts at 2 am on the last Sunday of September).
So please remember to adjust your clocks BACK 1 HOUR before you go to sleep on Saturday night.

DAYLIGHT SAVINGS PARTY
SAT 6 APRIL 6PM-3AM

DAYLIGHT SAVINGS PARTY starts at 6 pm on the first Saturday of April and ends at 3 am on Sunday which means...

【日本語】「何」にでも「首」を突っ込む→【英語】「すべてのパイ」に「指」を突っ込む

Some people cannot buy enough shoes, but others do not buy anything unless it makes them feel fabulous.

これで、オークランドのちょっとお洒落な「ことば散歩」はおしまいです。そして、ニュージーランドを舞台としたテキストもおしまいです。みなさんのなかで、ニュージーランドが、これまでよりも少し心近くなり、旅行や留学先にニュージーランドをえらんでみようかなと思っていただけたなら幸いです。もし、このテキストを片手に、オークランドの街歩きを楽しみながら、今度はご自分でことば散歩をしてみようかなという方が出てきてくだされば、筆者にとっても、キウイの国の人たちにとっても、これほど嬉しいことはありません。Ka kite ano!（またね！）

音声ファイルのダウンロード方法

英宝社ホームページ（http://www.eihosha.co.jp/）の
「テキスト音声ダウンロード」バナーをクリックすると、
音声ファイルダウンロードページにアクセスできます。

Cultural Crossroads
多文化の交差点 New Zealand

2020年1月15日　初　版

井　上　　　彰
共　著　者 © 今　泉　志　奈　子
Christopher Connelly

発　行　者　佐　々　木　　　元

発　行　所　株式
　　　　　　会社　英　　宝　　社
〒 101-0032 東京都千代田区岩本町 2-7-7
Tel ［03］（5833）5870　Fax ［03］（5833）5872

ISBN978-4-269-21000-4 C1082
［製版:㈱マナ・コムレード／表紙デザイン:興亜産業㈱／印刷・製本:モリモト印刷㈱］